CONNECTING CHURCH & SCHOOL
TEACHING THE BIBLE TO SCHOOL CHILDREN

CONNECTING CHURCH & SCHOOL

TEACHING THE BIBLE TO SCHOOL CHILDREN

Paul Coxall

RITCHIE
John Ritchie Publishing

40 Beansburn, Kilmarnock, Scotland

ISBN-13: 978 1 914273 37 7

Copyright © 2023 by John Ritchie Ltd.
40 Beansburn, Kilmarnock, Scotland

www.ritchiechristianmedia.co.uk

Typeset by John Ritchie Ltd., Kilmarnock
Printed by Bell & Bain Ltd., Glasgow

CONTENTS

INTRODUCTION

*"Give ear, O my people, to my law; incline your ears to the words of my mouth. I will open my mouth in a parable; I will utter dark sayings of old, which we have heard and known, and our fathers have told us. We will not hide them from their children, **telling to the generation to come the praises of the LORD, and His strength and His wonderful works that He has done"** (Psalm 78:1-4).*

*"Therefore you shall lay up these words of mine in your heart and in your soul, ... **You shall teach them to your children**, speaking of them when you sit in your house, when you walk by the way, when you lie down, and when you rise up"* (Deuteronomy 11:18-19).

*"**Whoever receives one of these little children in My name receives Me**; and whoever receives Me, receives not Me but Him who sent Me"* (Mark 9:37).

*"Then they brought little children to Him, that He might touch them; but the disciples rebuked those who brought them. But when Jesus saw it, He was greatly displeased and said to them, '**Let the little children come to Me**, and do not forbid them; for of such is the kingdom of God'"* (Mark 10:13-14).

Scripture clearly teaches that children should be taught the Word of God. Primarily this is the role of parents, that should commence when the child is very young. The home should be a place where the Scriptures are regularly read and discussed. Although the task is demanding it will be honoured by the Lord, who will never forget a work done in His name.

Someone has rightly said, "Mothers set the pattern, and then teach and train and discipline and influence the child to follow that same pattern in their own life".

Although there is a great responsibility placed on parents to teach their children, whom God has given to them, the truth about Himself and His plan of Salvation, the local church has a supporting role in this great task. Children should, as much as possible, be taken to the meetings of the Lord's people to hear the instruction from God's Word, join in the praising of His name and listen to the prayers of His people.

Countless adults have testified, in later life, that this practice in their early years, was formative and invaluable for them - although many of them were less than enthusiastic at the time!

Church-based youth clubs, Sunday schools and residential camps have also proven to be instrumental in being used by the Lord to bring children to faith in Jesus Christ.

However, as church attendance in the western world declines, there is a huge percentage of children who are not exposed to Christian teaching. In 1980 it was estimated that 11.8% of the UK population attended a church service, whereas in 2015 the figure was 5%. This figure is forecast to drop even further. The regularity of attendance by this small percentage is not known but it is indisputable that overall the number of adults and children attending church gatherings is sharply declining.

I am assuming that everyone who reads this book is concerned that many school-aged children do not know what the Bible has to say and has a desire to bring that good news to them. In a world full of different philosophies and ideologies, it is vitally important that the message of the Bible, a book that has transformed the lives of many as well as defining the laws and culture of numerous countries, is made known.

Many years ago, a servant of God said, *"Here am I! Send me"* (Isaiah 6:8b). Today there is a great need for believers to echo that same statement and to teach young children the wonderful message found in the Bible.

This book has been written, not by an expert, but someone who has endeavoured, through the local church, to develop a work in local schools. I have drawn on my experience and observations to offer guidance and advice to anyone who has a desire to serve the Lord by helping young children understand what the Bible teaches. Although the book is principally aimed at connecting with and teaching in Primary Schools (Children aged from 5-11 years old), I do hope it contains useful lessons for those looking to teach older children.

My prayer is that this book will be helpful and will offer encouragement to all who read it but especially those who desire to work with local schools and serve their children. If it achieves its purpose, then do thank the Lord. If there are errors or omissions, then do inform me but please forgive me.

CHAPTER 1
HOW IT STARTED v HOW'S IT GOING?

Having responded positively to the question, "Could you do the talk at the Youth Club next week?" I wondered what I might say to the children who came each week on a Monday night. I'd never spoken to such an audience before, but I had seen many people do it and as Christmas was only a fortnight away the theme for my talk was obvious.

Well, Monday night arrived. The usual activities took place and, after a time of enthusiastic singing, I was invited to come and speak. As I stood up, confidence deserted me. It was not that I had an abundant supply of it, but when I went to use my meagre resource, I found that it had departed.

As I looked at the rows of expectant faces, I momentarily considered a few options: running out of the hall would be a bit much but maybe a slight fainting episode would relieve me of this duty. As this thought raced through my mind, I considered that I could not and must not do such a thing, but I should carry on.

My eyes, once again, looked at the audience. I saw other adults who were more experienced and skilled at giving a children's talk. Now there were questions in my head: "What am I doing here? What will they think of me? Why should I do this?" My mind was racing but was not focused on the task before me.

So a nervous and unfocused young man stood up and read, from Matthew 2, about the Wise men who came to Jesus. After a very brief paraphrase of the story, I then made my main point (my only point!). "They came to worship Him", I said, "and so should we". That was it. I think the whole reading and talk lasted 3-4 minutes. The kindest verdict would be that it did not contain error and was not wearisome. In truth it lacked any explanation of who Jesus was, why He came, what is worship, how we can worship Him and why should we worship Him. I had missed a great opportunity to teach young children essential truths.

When I finished, there was a look of surprise on the young and less young faces. No-one had ever given such a brief talk. If there was a record for "shortest talk ever", then I was now in first place with a time that would stand for decades. One of my fellow leaders, whilst trying to hide his amazed and perplexed reaction, suggested we sing a few more choruses. After all, there was at least another 10 minutes until the end of the club.

My debut at speaking to children was, to put it mildly, not a great success. My answering machine (this was pre-mobile phone era) was not inundated with invitations for further talks and I knew that there was huge room for improvement.

That infamous (in my mind) Monday night was nearly 30 years ago. That's 'How it started' but let me tell you 'How it's going'.

By God's grace, I now teach in 8-9 primary schools, to children in the P5-P7 age range, a programme called 'Explore the Essentials'. This course has 24 lessons, delivered over 2 academic years, that cover the main events and characters of the Bible. In the goodness of God, He has given me a wonderful privilege of serving Him by teaching in primary school classrooms. Through 'Explore the Essentials' approximately 750 children annually receive 10-12 hours of Bible teaching, delivered in accordance with the school curriculum.

In addition, I have the honour of taking school assemblies, hosting a Bible Exhibition and co-ordinating a calendar competition with local schools. Along with youth club talks and other children's ministry there has been a lot of change (and hopefully some improvement) over the last 30 years.

In this book I want to share my experience and learnings, so that you might be helped in children's work, particularly in engaging with and serving local schools. I would like to share how, by the Lord's leading, I arrived in my current situation, but I understand this is not necessarily the exact path you will walk. Each of us is unique and the path where our wise heavenly Father leads us will be different and suited for what He requires of us. Although every believer has the same destination, the course that is set out for us is unique.

I hope my testimony to His leading will encourage and stimulate your service for Him.

I cannot recall my next invitation after the short debut, but undoubtedly gracious and patient leaders gave me further opportunities to speak to children. A later chapter, in this book, will look at the subject of training but suffice to say I did learn, albeit slowly.

Through serving regularly at weekly youth clubs and residential camps, I was able to *stir up the gift of God"* (2 Timothy 1:6) so that I might be more useful in His service. Back then I had no idea of where the Lord would lead me. If you had told me that, years later, I would give up paid employment to develop and deliver a Bible teaching programme to young children, I would not have believed you.

Looking back, I can see that a significant moment was the hosting of a Bible Exhibition at our church, in the early 2000s. A later chapter will give more details about hosting a Bible Exhibition to help connect with local schools.

One significant feature of the Exhibition was that the children completed an activity worksheet during their visit, and we promised them that the best worksheets would receive a prize. Once the worksheets were marked and the winners selected, I contacted the schools and arranged a prize-giving assembly. These events would be my first venture outside the relative safety of a church building or environment. We chose a suitable Bible-based book as a prize and had the winner's name written inside by an expert calligrapher (maybe that's not the title he would use but it was a man with very neat writing who owned an ink pen).

Thankfully, for my listeners, after many years of practice at youth clubs, I was able to deliver a suitable talk to the whole school. Knowing what classes would be present, how long I had to speak for, what facilities were available and what time the assembly was helped in the preparation phase. Once again, a later chapter will give more details about speaking at a school assembly.

As in many areas of life, building and strengthening relationships is vital. Speaking to the Head Teacher or Deputy Head and asking genuine questions meant I was able to understand more about the school. During our conversation or in an email of thanks I would always offer to take further assemblies. Over a period of time, every school responded positively to this offer and slowly I built up a network of contacts in local primary schools and took assemblies on a regular basis. If the school did not respond to an initial offer, I would follow up with offers to take Christmas or Easter assemblies.

With a flexible work situation, I was able to take time off work for a school assembly and then make up the time later in the day or week. However, with increasing activity in local schools and other areas of ministry I had reached a point where I could not do any more school work and also have a full-time job in the Oil and Gas industry.

I had often thought about giving up paid employment to devote more time to the other ministries the Lord had called me to but was very unsure. "Surely this work would be for the super-spiritual?", "Are you just thinking this because you're tired of completing monthly sales forecasts?", "What will others think?", "There's others more gifted than you" were some of the doubts and questions that filled my head. Prayer helped greatly but one prayer did not answer all my doubts and questions. However, I can testify that the Lord did provide all the answers I needed and placed an increasing burden on me to start a new chapter in service for Him.

In the late summer of 2018, I was led to leave the Oil and Gas industry and venture into a new area. One lunchtime I was reading Joshua 1. The words of verse 9, *" Have I not commanded you? Be strong and of good courage; do not be afraid, nor be dismayed, for the LORD your God is with you wherever you go"*, struck me as if they were being spoken directly to me.

Unlike Joshua, I was not being called to take a people into the promised land, but just like him I was being called into a new area, unsure of how it would develop but certain that the Lord wanted me to be strong and have courage.

So, in October 2018, I left paid employment and, with the full support of my local assembly, entered a new phase of the Lord's work. The details of how I would engage with local schools more deeply were unknown to me. I had researched what other people were doing in primary school work and found that very useful as I formulated some ideas. After a time of prayer and discussions with a few teachers, the idea of a course that would teach the main events and characters in Christianity began to crystallize in my mind.

In Scotland, all schools must teach in accordance with the Curriculum for Excellence (CfE) and Christianity is specifically mentioned in the Religious and Moral Education section. With this knowledge, I wrote down a rough outline for teaching 24 lessons over a 2-year period. I wanted to teach the big story of the Bible with 12 lessons each from the Old and New Testaments. I quickly realised I would need to write a detailed lesson plan for each of the 24 lessons and would need to work hard on varying the teaching methods. The teachers would need to see a lesson plan and the pupils would engage better with varied lessons.

To cut a long story short, I managed to write a lesson plan for a sample lesson and included that in an overview document for the course that I had named, 'Explore the Essentials'. In early 2019, I approached some of the primary schools that I had taken assemblies in and explained this new area of service that could help them deliver the requirements of the CfE. I was conscious that this would be a huge step for the headteacher in the primary schools. Having a volunteer teach in the classroom every week is quite different from someone speaking at the occasional school assembly.

However, the Lord opened doors of opportunity. Undoubtedly due to relationships of trust that had been built up and strengthened over many years, a few schools invited me to take lessons. So, in February 2019 I entered a primary school classroom for the first time in 45 years. The first lessons on Creation were well received and provoked questions from the children. I found an interactive style of teaching helped engage the children, as I would ask them questions and get them to read from a whiteboard. In those early years, I worked to produce classroom exercises that would reinforce the teaching I was giving. The floor of my study was frequently covered with laminated cards and worksheets. A laminating machine, printer and paper trimmer guillotine were essential tools in preparing lesson material.

Once I had delivered lessons to a few schools, I approached other schools and informed them what I was doing and how I could help. What I was doing elsewhere provided reassurance to these schools. One of them even phoned another one for a review of my work. For the 2019/2020 school year, I taught the P5 and P6 pupils in 8 local primary schools. When I left paid employment in October 2018 my plan was not entirely clear, but the Lord did make the way clear, opened doors and gave huge opportunities that I could not imagine.

That is a summary of "How it started v How it's going". Countless people continually discover that the Lord can use and equip the most unlikely of people - and I am certainly proof of that!

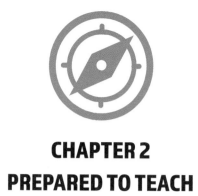

CHAPTER 2
PREPARED TO TEACH

I'm confident every reader of this book does want to teach God's Word well to children. You would not be reading this book if that were not the case! You may not be the best teacher, but you want to do what you can to improve and help others to improve.

Preparation

Preparation is a key element in service. An old adage states, "Failing to prepare is preparing to fail". This is true in many areas of life and particularly in the teaching of God's Word, no matter the age and size of the audience. Turning up and hoping to "Wing it" as it is "only a children's talk" is not suitable preparation, dishonours the Lord and is disrespectful to those who will listen.

As an aeroplane has two wings that are essential for flight to take place, so there are two essential aspects for proper preparation.

One is dependence upon the Lord in prayer. Prayer is often neglected but it is crucial in teaching God's Word. We must look to Him to direct us in the use of words and phrases that are true to His Word and understandable to the listeners. As you read the passage (You will do this a few times), ask Him to illuminate your mind to grasp the central truths and how it points to Christ. Trust that the Holy Spirit will guide you as you speak. Only He can open the blind eyes, give light where there is darkness and bring the dead to life, so we must rely upon Him to do the work that only He can do.

Although many of us want to get on with 'real work', we must have an increasing realisation that the words of the Lord Jesus, *"for without Me you can do nothing"* (John 15:5), do apply in all areas of ministry where we want to be fruitful for Him. It greatly helps us when we understand that prayer is real work. It is hard but it is essential.

The second essential aspect of preparation is studying for and planning the lesson. You will need to know some practical details. How long will your part in the lesson or assembly last for? What age of children will be present? What facilities are available for visual and audio projection? Is there time for a quiz or singing?

You will need to decide upon the Biblical passage or theme that you will speak about. If a school has asked you to incorporate one of their core values, such as kindness, fairness, respect, love, or honesty, into the lesson, you will need to think how this can be done fairly and accurately. Thankfully, many of the values we have in the western world are drawn from our Judeo-Christian heritage, so aligning a school value with a Biblical story should not be an insurmountable task.

If there is a special occasion occurring, then you could use that as a basis for a lesson. Christmas, Easter, and Harvest thanksgiving are often celebrated in school, so introducing the clear Bible message on these occasions is appropriate. Events like the Olympics, World Cup, School sports day etc can be a helpful pathway that would help you introduce a scriptural lesson. On occasion, you might like to consider a biographical talk on the life of a Christian. The stories of people like Eric Liddell, Jim Elliot, Mary Jones and Amy Carmichael are fascinating for children (and adults) and can be used to explain what they believed and did as a result of that belief. Good graphics are readily available for many biographical lessons.

Once a theme or passage is decided upon, then you will need to carefully consider how you will present this. I have dealt with communication already but suffice to say that you will need to think what the big point is that you want to deliver, what will be emphasised and what can be left out for the sake of clarity and time. Writing an outline is, in my opinion, vitally important. This will help you see if there is a good structure and will clarify your thinking. Your outline will help you see if you have covered what needs to be expressed. If you are anything like me, you will need to constantly work on simplicity and clarity when speaking to children.

Another consideration is the use of visual aids. Using these has proved to be very beneficial in teaching young children but do remember it is an aid, designed to help you teach the truth. So, don't let the aid became the lesson. When I first started in youth clubs, PowerPoint was not invented. Flannelgraphs and acetates (you might need to Google that!) were the common tools that people used. The talented artist could use a sketch board and there was always the use of an object lesson. All of these, except for acetates that require an overhead projector (another Google project!), can still be used.

One example of using object lessons is a talk on the Bible. I have a small black bag containing a light, bread, a sword (envelope opener), seeds and a mirror. Giving a clue, I ask the children to guess an item that is in the bag and then, once they have guessed it, proceed to tell them how the Bible uses that as a simile to describe itself. Although I may not use the word 'simile', I can tell them that the Bible is a light to our path, food for our souls, a sword that cuts deep, a seed that can bring fruit and a mirror that shows us what we are like. Object lessons can help illustrate Biblical truth.

Nowadays, there are a huge variety of high-quality images that can be used on presentation software such as PowerPoint. Most schools have projectors in the classroom and the assembly hall. Using a laptop to present means that you can show pictures to a large audience. This would not be realistic if using a flannelgraph. Having spoken to large school assemblies with 100s of children in attendance, I do appreciate a large screen which can display images of the lesson I am giving.

If you have never used one of these presentation methods, then do prepare by practising at home. You may get some friends to give feedback or maybe some young children.

Prepare well and you will most likely deliver well.

Training

When we examine the life of the Apostles, we can clearly see that they spent 3 years with the Lord Jesus being trained by Him for the work they would do once He ascended to heaven. Likewise the Apostle Paul trained young Timothy for a great work, and we can see from 2 Timothy 2 verse 2 that passing on the truth and training did not stop at Timothy: *"And the things that you have heard from me among many witnesses, commit these to faithful men who will be able to teach others also"*.

Letting a complete novice, without any formal or any informal training, teach God's Word to any audience is somewhat foolish. It is hard to think of an area in public life where this would be seen as suitable. If my car needs to be serviced, I'm hopeful the mechanic who will do the work is not just keen but has been trained. As the hearts and minds of children are much more important than my car, there should be some training for those who will instruct them.

This training need not be formal, although it could be. It should not be solely based in a classroom. Training in some form is vital. Scottish friends may recognise the phrase, *"Some things are better felt than telt"*, which could roughly be translated as, *"Some things are better caught than taught"*. By observing someone closely, we can often learn more about a subject than if we read a book about it.

In the area of speaking to school children, weekly youth clubs and Sunday schools can be a great training ground for those who will speak to youngsters. Over the course of months and years, the keen novice should be able to learn from observing and speaking to those more proficient than they are. Experienced leaders should be intentional in giving guidance and training to those who desire and require it. Although this will take time and effort from both parties, it will be energy well spent. The trainee will need to be humble enough to receive advice and the more competent will need to be patient and tolerant in giving it. Asking questions will be a important feature of a fruitful partnership, so both parties must be committed to that.

Regarding training, a prerequisite is a God-given desire to serve Him by bringing His Word to children. Someone may ask, "How can I know if my desires are from the Lord?" The answer to that noble question is not to be found in looking for mystical signs or secret messages in Scripture. If your life has a pattern of taking pleasure in all that the Lord is and does, then God promises that the desires in your heart are from Him.

"Delight yourself also in the LORD, and He shall give you the desires of your heart" (Psalm 37:4).

> ## "A good working knowledge of the Bible is something that every believer will pursue."

Delighting in the Lord means our desire will be for more of Him, to know Him better and to serve Him in ways that are pleasing to Him. Undoubtedly teaching children His Word is pleasing to Him.

If we have a desire to teach children, then an essential foundation is a good working knowledge of the Bible. If we do not know our subject, then it is impossible to teach it well. We want to tell children the truth and not our version of it.

A good working knowledge of the Bible is something that every believer will pursue. Along with a discipleship model of the inexperienced being actively guided and taught by someone more experienced, I would also recommend obtaining some good books on teaching children.

The best resource that I obtained, nearly 25 years ago, is the **'Children's Ministry Resource Bible'**. This Bible combines the New King James Version with very useful teaching aids from an organisation called 'Child Evangelism Fellowship'. On the first pages of this Bible you will find the classic Wordless Book with helpful instructions on how to present the Gospel whilst using this very simple visual aid.

One of the best features of this book is the detailed plans provided for many lessons that might be given to children. All 104 plans have symbols that indicate when a truth about God, Sin, the Cross, Jesus Christ, or a Challenge could be taught. The reader will find this method in lesson preparation very effective. There are many articles, including how to teach children, how to prepare a lesson and early childhood education principles.

This Resource Bible is a great tool for anyone who desires to teach children.

Another area for training is for the local church to host a training day, or half-day, for anyone with a desire to reach and teach youngsters. The more experienced can share observations and experiences with the less experienced. Alternatively a speaker could be invited to provide and facilitate learning. This type of experience can be stimulating and educational for all.

Training is an ongoing process that should be encouraged and is an area that I would heartily endorse.

CHAPTER 3
CONNECTION

Making and maintaining connections with local schools is vital. It can be hard work and often takes a considerable amount of time and perseverance. Once there is a connection, as with all relationships, the subsequent preserving and strengthening of them does not happen without significant effort.

Many Christians see a great need to serve local schools and help youngsters. Although a relationship cannot be established and thrive if the effort is solely in one direction, making a connection with a local school will require considerable endeavour by a local assembly. I would like to share some of the ways that I have proved to be successful in linking with local schools. Most of my experience and observations are within Primary Schools (for ages 5-11 years old) but I am convinced that many of these ideas are transferrable to Secondary Schools (12-17 years old).

Parent Councils

There may be different names in other geographical locations but in Scotland (the country where I reside) every school should have a parent forum and a parent council. Membership of a parent forum consists of parents who have a child at a local authority school. One of the ways parents in the parent forum can serve and express their views is through the parent council.

The function of a parent council is to provide a voice for parents in schools and in their local authority on issues that are important to them. Additionally, they should promote contact between the school and the local community.

If you have a child of school-age, then you should consider serving on the parent council. There may be valid reasons as to why you are unable to but serving the school in this way could have multiple benefits, including promoting contact between the school and the local church. Relationships of trust can also be developed through this work. When a school is approached by a local church, it is beneficial if they know the person who is communicating with them. Would you trust your children to someone you had never met?

You will require wisdom in this area of service, but you can look to the promise of God for this.

"If any of you lacks wisdom, let him ask of God, who gives to all liberally and without reproach, and it will be given to him" (James 1:5).

Bible Exhibitions

This area of ministry was my first exposure to children's work with schools. Although I had been involved in church youth groups and residential camps, hosting a Bible Exhibition was a new venture as it involved directly communicating with schools.

The basic premise of most Bible Exhibitions is to invite local primary school classes to your church hall, or other facility, for a tour of an exhibition about the Bible. Over the course of a week approximately 15 classes of 9-11 years old children are given an overview of the Bible's importance and message. A class of pupils can be divided into 4-5 groups and a local church member will guide the children round. Usually the tour is concluded with a fun quiz and light refreshments, when the

" ... the exhibition provides opportunities for Christians to work together."

4-5 groups come together. As they depart, a gift pack, with appropriate Bible literature, could be given.

It is vitally important to inform the school, when you invite them, of everything that will take place in the visit. They will not appreciate a gift pack being given if you have not informed them beforehand.

As well as serving the local schools and making the message of the gospel known, the exhibition provides opportunities for Christians to work together. You will need a suitable hall and volunteers for a variety of roles

One of the key features of an effective exhibition is the ability to facilitate ongoing engagement with the local schools. A worksheet that the children complete as they are guided can be marked and a visit to the school for a prizegiving assembly can be organised. As the school has visited a Bible Exhibition, there should be no surprise or concern when the prize is related to the Bible. Of course, informing the school beforehand of what you will be awarding as a prize is best practice.

My first visits to schools were for this type of assembly and from them further invitations were given.

As the local assembly provides transportation and resources, there is no financial cost to the school. In times of budget cuts this can be a great help for any school. The exhibition provides an out of school experience for the children, covers teaching that is mandatory in the school curriculum and provides contact with the local community.

Hosting a Bible Exhibition on an annual basis is a great way to engage with local schools. A small start can develop into something bigger.

Lunchtime clubs

I do not know of any schools that do not have lunchtime clubs. Although they are time limited (30 minutes is the usual length), they offer youngsters an opportunity to engage in an alternative activity during their lunchbreak.

Scripture Union (SU) are a well-known organisation who facilitate a wide range of activities for children. Often a school will have heard of SU and you may find doors open more easily and that you have access to good support if you run an SU club in a school.

If you have a desire to run a lunchtime club, then do research on what clubs the school already runs. There's little point in duplicating what is already offered. If there is no Bible-based lunchtime club, do contact the school to explain how you would like to help them. As with all communication, speaking face to face is the preferred format (1Thessalonians 3:6) but failing that an email with a phone call follow up would be my advice. Be clear on what you will be doing and what age-range the club is for.

As some schools have staggered lunchtimes, you may not be able to reach your target age range, but having a club for all primary school ages (4–11 years old) would not be advisable. Targeting a few upper or lower primary school years will mean you can structure the activities accordingly. In a secondary school, you may be able to invite a wider age range.

Having a small team of volunteers is desirable for this weekly activity, not just for the help during the club but for ideas on what to do at the club. Standing up, each week, and giving a 30-minute talk will probably ensure your lunchtimes are quickly free for alternative activities! Giving thought into how to vary the content and ensure youngsters are engaged will be hard but satisfying work.

The school will need to provide you with a suitable room, and you will need to have a safeguarding check and possibly complete the school's own training.

Lunchtime clubs require commitment and perseverance but can be a great way to allow youngsters to hear the gospel and connect with the local school.

After-school clubs

Much of what has been written above can apply to after-school clubs. Co-ordinating with the school, a club that is run once the school day finishes can be a great help for parents of younger children who will appreciate coming to collect them a bit later than normal.

One practical aspect is that registration for the club and notifying parents if a child has not turned up needs to be rigorously controlled. If a parent thinks their child is at a club but the child has left the school grounds, there could be unwanted repercussions.

One additional aspect that should be considered for an after-school club is for it to be based on a hobby or pastime, such as running or singing. Although it will not be a club that directly proclaims Biblical truth, it will be a good work that will serve others and be valued by the school. As well as helping youngsters in a meaningful way, the relationship of trust will be built with the school.

After an afternoon of Bible teaching, in a local primary school, I lead an after-school running club that is well subscribed. There is a range of ability at this club, but I am pleased to see youngsters getting physical exercise and enjoying a gift that God has given them.

Assemblies

As of 2022, assemblies are still held in most UK schools. Current law requires all state-funded schools in England, Wales, and Northern Ireland to hold daily acts of 'Collective Worship'. In England and Wales in schools with no formal religious character, this worship must be 'wholly or mainly of a broadly Christian character'. In Northern Ireland the requirement is for 'undenominational' collective worship. In Scotland, The Education (Scotland) Act 1980 sets out that, in all state-funded schools, the practice of 'religious observance' should occur, unless a resolution to discontinue this has been passed by the local education authority and approved by the electors in that local authority area. Scottish Government Guidance is that it should take place at least six times a year.

If you have a desire to serve by taking a school assembly, I would not advise contacting the school reminding them of the law. Such an approach will not be well received and is very unlikely to gain you an invitation. Contacting the school and offering your help in this area will, hopefully, be well received.

Once again having a relationship with the Headteacher or whoever organises the assembly will be valuable. Assemblies for special occasions (Christmas, Easter, Harvest thanksgiving, local events) might be the best option for someone contacting a school for the first time. Alternatively, you could research the school's values, aims or core values from their website. Then, once you have designed a Bible-based assembly on one aspect, you could approach the school with your proposal. A clear plan of what you are going to talk about will be greatly appreciated.

Advice on communication and presentation in the assembly is given in another chapter of this book.

Bible presentations

For many years the Gideons, now called 'Good News for Everyone' (GNfE) in the UK, have sought to present Bibles to every school child. Along with many helpful notes the Bible that the children are offered contains the New Testament, Psalms, and Proverbs.

Most commonly the offer of a Bible is made at a school assembly to those in the first year of secondary school. Although there is no obligation for a school to host such an assembly, many do respond positively.

Approaching GNfE (goodnewsuk.com) would be an advisable first step in ascertaining if this type of assembly takes place at the secondary schools in your area. If you find out that this offer is not taking place in your community, then you could either offer to help GNfE in this ministry or undertake it yourself.

If after approaching local secondary schools in a gracious and wise manner, you do not find an 'open door', then you could approach the local primary schools and offer to take an assembly or classroom presentation for their final year pupils.

There are many testimonies of how a Bible, presented at school, has in later years been opened and transformed that person's life and destiny. Here's one inspiring testimony.

"My name is Pamela and I want to share my gratitude for the small red Bible I received from Irvine Royal Academy. I received my Bible from yourselves when I was 12, in my first year at secondary school around 20 years ago. I wrote my name in it and kept it by my bed, occasionally picking it up but never really knowing where to start... One day during a clear out, I found the small red Bible I was given at school ... That day I opened it and read the introduction then started with the 30 day readings. From that day I have read it every morning and sometimes more when I feel I need that extra time with God. It has answered many of my questions and has helped make things clear to me from the last 17 years. The answers truly are in God's Word.

Thank you for that gift to a small, quiet 12-year-old who never knew until her 30s exactly the power that was put into her hands."

Classroom lessons

I have written elsewhere in this book, how the Lord guided me and opened doors of opportunity that mean I am currently teaching the truths of Christianity, in school classrooms, to 9–11 year-old children on a regular basis. As I am not a registered teacher with the necessary qualifications, a teacher is always present in the classroom with me.

In UK schools the curriculum does call for some form of religious education that must include Christianity. As of 2022 the Scottish Curriculum for Excellence includes outcomes such as:

- Christianity – Beliefs - Through exploring the lives and teachings of Jesus and other figures in Christianity, I am increasing my knowledge and understanding of key Christian beliefs. - RME 2-01b

- Christianity - Values and issues - Second Level – (P5-P7) - Through investigating and reflecting upon the lives and teachings of Jesus and key Christian figures, and drawing upon moral values as expressed in Christianity, I am beginning to understand how these have influenced Christian morality. - RME 2-02a

- Christianity - Practices and traditions - Second Level – (P5-P7) - I can describe the practices and traditions of Christianity and have considered the way these have influenced Scottish society. - RME 2-03c

As this teaching is mandated in schools, there does exist an opportunity for a believer to serve the school by teaching on a voluntary basis. This could be for one-off lessons at certain times of the year or for a short series.

Before approaching a school, I would strongly advise that you have a lesson plan for what you will teach. A robust plan will demonstrate that you have thought about the structure and content of the lesson. Additionally, you should think about any cross-curriculum content that can be included. Now, that might sound somewhat daunting, so let me expand on that. Although Christianity is the main theme of your talk you could incorporate some other subjects. A few examples are provided below:

- Noah's Ark – In this talk you could take a tape measure and explain what a cubit was. Once they know it was the distance between the elbow and the top of the middle fingertip, you could ask them to calculate the dimensions of the ark in metres, as you have given them measurements in cubits. To make this easier I always use 0.5m as approximately equal to 1 cubit.

- Tower of Babel – Once you have told them why we have different languages, then explain that the people needed to develop a written language. Show how many words in Chinese show that the ancient Chinese knew the Gospel message found in the book of Genesis. They can then draw some of these Chinese characters. There are a few examples at www.answersingenesis.org/genesis/chinese-characters-and-genesis. Make sure you research this and practise before the lesson.

- Good Samaritan – In this lesson the great shock, to the original hearers, was that the one who helped was a Samaritan. Racism and prejudice are not new so you could ask the class to think when we have seen it in history. I show suitable pictures from World War II, the Suffragettes and Apartheid in South Africa.

For many lessons I produce worksheets that include coded puzzles or wordsearches that they must solve to reveal a Bible verse. For younger children, you could do more craft-based activities.

Imagination and initiative can be used to construct accurate and enjoyable lessons for the pupils.

An example lesson plan, based on the Scottish Curriculum for Excellence, is shown on the following pages.

Second Level – (P5-P7) - The Flood

Stage	Second Level – (P5-P7)
Rationale	Understanding the Biblical teaching on the global flood account. We will seek to understand this occurred and what was the impact on the world.
People involved	Pupils over a course of 45-minute classroom sessions.
Learning intentions	The pupils will understand the biblical account of the Flood narrative. The concepts of sin, warning, grace and promise will be emphasized. They will also calculate the size of the ark using biblical dimensions.
Links with Curriculum for Excellence	**Religious and moral education: experiences and outcomes** Through investigating and reflecting upon biblical and other Christian stories, I can show my understanding of these stories. - RME 2-01a Through exploring the lives and teachings of Jesus and other figures in Christianity, I am increasing my knowledge and understanding of key Christian beliefs. -RME 2-01b I can show understanding of Christian beliefs and explore the similarities and differences between these and my developing beliefs. - RME 2-01c I can share my developing views about values such as fairness and equality and love, caring, sharing and human rights. - RME 2-02b **Literacy and Numeracy: experiences and outcomes** When I engage with others, I can respond in ways appropriate to my role, show that I value others' contributions and use these to build on thinking. - LIT 2-02a I can recognise how the features of spoken language can help in communication, and I can use what I learn. I can recognise different features of my own and others' spoken language. - ENG 2-03a I can show my understanding of what I listen to or watch by responding to literal, inferential, evaluative and other types of questions, and by asking different kinds of questions of my own. - LIT 2-07a I am developing confidence when engaging with others within and beyond my place of learning. I can communicate in a clear, expressive way and I am learning to select and organise resources independently. - LIT 2-10a / LIT 3-10a I can use the common units of measure, convert between related units of the metric system and carry out calculations when solving problems. - MNU 2-11b

Second Level - (P5-P7) - The Flood

The Lesson

Introduction (5 minutes)
- From EfE 3 we will consider the subject of 'Grace'. What is grace and how did God show grace to Noah?

Storytelling and poster work (30 minutes)
- The biblical account of the Flood story will be told. The subjects of sin, judgment, grace and promise will be discussed. I will be using pictures and will ask the children to read aloud some passage from the Bible. (PC and Screen/Projector).
- The children will engage with the story by being asked to **calculate the size of the Ark**.
- The children will engage with the story by thinking about warnings we receive.
- The children will reflect on promises that are made, the different types that are made and why sometimes we do not keep them.
- The relationship between Noah's Ark and how it points to Jesus Christ will be introduced.

Key points from the story:
- Mankind rebelled against God.
- God said He would punish mankind for breaking the rules.
- God provided a way of escape, salvation.
- God did judge in exactly the way He promised.
- After the flood God made a promise.

Think and discuss (5 minutes)
- Was it fair that there was a global flood?
- Did God have to provide a way of escape?

Dig deeper or review (10 minutes)
- The children will be given a simple worksheet to complete. This will involve drawing a line between a question and pictorial answer,

  And/or
- The children will be asked to look at a worksheet with conditional and unconditional promises and seek to identify them. They will also be asked to write their own conditional promise and an unconditional one.

Competition (5 minutes) - if time allows
Quiz
True or False - There will be posters at either end of the classroom and the children will go to one of them to answer the question.

One other area that you should consider for classroom lessons are the resources produced by Bible Education Services (www. besweb.com/about-bibletime/).

Bible Education Services have written and published an extensive range of Bible courses and lessons. Their Bibletime series has 5 ability levels with suggested age guides from Pre-school to 14+. There is a 3-year syllabus for each level, which means that a child could complete a unique lesson every week for 15 years.

These resources are used throughout the world and can be used in UK classrooms. The lessons are also available in other languages.

Calendars

A great opportunity to engage with local schools is in the production of calendar. Through a calendar project local school children have an opportunity to provide a picture for one of the months and receive a prize.

The concept is that templates are delivered to local schools for all the 6-11 year old children to complete. There will be 12 different templates with enough delivered to the school so that each eligible child has one. The children then colour the templates and submit to the school. All the templates are collected and then the best one of each template is selected. These are then scanned in and sent to a designer who can incorporate them into a yearly calendar. Once the design has been completed, it is sent to a printer who will produce the finished article.

The finished calendars are then taken to the participating schools. The prizegiving assembly for the template winners can take place. The school usually give a calendar to all pupils and staff.

Shown below is one of the winning templates we have used in this high-quality calendar.

We know that many calendars are displayed in homes and shops in the community and one significant reason is because local children have contributed to the production. Here's the back cover to a recent calendar.

An example timeline and 2022 budgetary costs are shown below.

- 1st week in October – Contact schools about the calendar project and ask them if they would like to participate. Six local schools join with us, so we can select 2 winners from each school.

- 2nd week in October – Design 12 templates, using clipart pictures and a font that can be coloured in by children. Have enough templates printed so that every eligible child can have one.

- Week after October school holidays – Deliver the templates to the schools. Having them in bundles of 24-30 would be helpful for classroom distribution.

- Early November – Collect the completed templates from the schools. The hard part is then selecting the 12 successful templates. Ensure the schools are represented fairly in this selection and do make allowances for differing abilities due to age. The templates can be scanned and saved as JPEGs.

- Mid November – Send the JPEGs to a designer whom you will have previously spoken to about the calendar. I use and would recommend Stewart Rollo (stewart@therollos.co.uk).

- Mid November – Submit the final design to a printer. I use and would recommend Quinns Printers (www.quinnstheprinters.com/products/calendars). A high quality calendar would be an A4 Calendar with 28 pages, 300gsm cover and 170gsm silk inners that is hole drilled.

- Early December – Calendars are delivered to you.

- Early to Mid-December - Delivery and presentation of calendars at the school.

The budgetary costs for 2,000 high quality calendars are:

- Design of A4 templates – Free, as hopefully you can do this or know someone who can.

- Printing of 2,000 A4 templates - £100.

- Scanning of templates – Free. Once again this can be done by yourself or someone you know.

- Design of the whole calendar and production of print-ready PDF - £200

- Printing of 2,000 Calendars - £1,400

- Prizes for 12 Children - £200

Therefore the total budget for this project is under £2,000. Each calendar costs less than £1 and is a superb outreach tool that you can use to engage with local schools.

Material Aid projects

Undoubtedly the focus of the local assembly should be to obey the commission that the Lord Jesus Christ gave:

"Go therefore and make disciples of all the nations, baptizing them in the name of the Father and of the Son and of the Holy Spirit, teaching them to observe all things that I have commanded you; and lo, I am with you always, even to the end of the age" (Matthew 28:19-20).

There should be a desire to see people, of all ages, come to know Jesus Christ as their Saviour, having repented of sin, and confessed that He is Lord. Discipleship then continues as every believer grows in conformity to the Lord. In summary the objective should be "To know Christ and make Him known".

To know Christ and to make Him known."

How this is accomplished can take many paths, some of which have been outlined in this book.

There are always opportunities for assemblies to be involved in materially helping those in need. Someone once summarised the Christian's concern as, *"Christians care about all suffering, especially eternal suffering".*

Although the local church needs to take care that it is not, or does not become, a 'social work' centre that reduces the proclamation of the gospel to a side issue, it should be involved in helping others with material needs.

The book of James reminds us that those with a living faith will want to help others.

"If a brother or sister is naked and destitute of daily food, and one of you says to them, "Depart in peace, be warmed and filled," but you do not give them the things which are needed for the body, what does it profit? Thus also faith by itself, if it does not have works, is dead" (James 2:15-17).

One area that can be overlooked or ignored is inviting schools to participate in material aid projects. When the assembly seeks to help others with material aid then consider, when appropriate, inviting local schools to participate in the project. Usually a well-organised and meaningful project will be well received in the local community.

This will be an area where you can establish deeper engagement with schools in the community, building up trust and displaying care.

There are a huge variety of worthwhile aid projects, and discernment is required as to what you should be involved in. As in many areas of ministry, the list of what you could do and what you should do will be different, the latter being shorter than the former. Consider aid parcels to missionaries or missionary support organisations, Christmas parcels for children at home or abroad, food boxes for the poor and relief for those impacted by war or famine.

Conclusion

This chapter summarises several areas that could help you engage with schools in your community. Consider those that may be suitable for your locality and the resources that you have, bring this matter before the Lord in prayer and He will direct your path.

"Trust in the LORD with all your heart, and lean not on your own understanding; In all your ways acknowledge Him, and He shall direct your paths" (Proverbs 3:5-6).

CHAPTER 3
COMMUNICATION

Communicating effectively is extremely important. Young children need to hear words and phrases that they can understand or can have quickly and accurately explained to them. Although verbal proclamation is the primary method of communication, we also communicate with body language. How we use our eyes, our hands and even our body shape communicates a message.

Whatever visual aids we use should also help communicate a clear message. The key feature of a visual aid should be the fact that it aids the presentation of God's Word. Most often PowerPoint presentations can be very helpful in school assemblies or classrooms, but other visual aids can be very effective in teaching young children.

Verbal communication

Firstly, I want to consider verbal interaction. For many people, going into a school for the first time will bring a sense of trepidation. Nerves and anxiety about what to say, what not to say and how to say it could be overwhelming. The environment is different from a church setting and although the Bible's message does not change, how we present it will need some adjustment.

> **A good introduction will grab the attention of the audience."**

Good verbal communication will start with your arrival at the school. A smile, eye engagement and a sincere greeting to all staff, from the receptionist whom you first meet as you register to the person who will be hosting the assembly or lesson is basic good manners. Usually the person hosting the assembly will ask how they should introduce you. I have never heard a staff member being referred to as anything but their surname. My preference has always been to be addressed as 'Paul' and that's how I'm greeted in every school I visit. That is matter of your personal preference and either form is acceptable.

Being ready ahead of time will communicate a message to staff and children. Arriving at the venue in plenty of time with all your required material is a minimum requirement and anything less than that would be seen as disrespectful.

When it comes to your lesson, I always greet the classroom or assembly with a smile and a greeting. "Good morning, everyone" usually elicits an enthusiastic response of, "Good morning, Paul".

Introduction

A good introduction to your talk will grab the attention of the audience. This is true when teaching adults but even more so when speaking to children. Try and think of a few lines that will make a child want to sit up and listen. If you are comfortable and it is suitable, you could ask a question and receive a few answers from the children.

Remember that keeping the attention of the children is a skill that can be learnt with practice although even the best communicators cannot hold every child's attention.

I have compiled a few of my introductions as examples for you. Once you have reviewed these, I am sure better ones will form in your mind.

- "Imagine there was a birth that was so special, the calendar was based on that event!" – The Birth of the Lord Jesus – There's no need to mention that those who originally determined the year got it wrong by 4-5 years. I would just say that the originally calculated date was used as the basis for our calendar.

- "Who is your greatest sporting hero?" – Biography talk on Eric Liddell – This question will usually produce a large variety of responses and I will then tell them who mine is and why. Biographical talks are a great tool for proclaiming the gospel as you can preface everything with phrases like, "Eric believed what the Bible said about ..." or "Eric believed ...".

- "Today we are going to look at the amazing story of a really disobedient and disrespectful young man." – The Prodigal Son - Most, if not all the children, will know someone who would fit this description and will be interested to hear what happens to him.

- "I'm sure you all show kindness to your friends, but what about those who are very different from us? Do we show the same kindness to them?" – The Good Samaritan – This lesson could emphasise a school value such as 'kindness'. You can then show how we should kindness to those who are quite different from us. To avoid this just being a good moral lesson you could then say how the Bible presents Jesus as the great example of kindness to those who were different from Him, by dying on the cross for them.

Verbal content

As in all cases of public speaking, it is good to know the audience. In a UK primary school setting, unless you know different, do assume there will be very little Bible knowledge. Therefore, do not use terms, without careful explanation, that would be unfamiliar to the children. Additionally do not try and include every detail that you know. It will be better to emphasise a few points very well than incorporating every fact and doctrinal point. Children who, metaphorically, need a glass of water will not benefit from a fire hose on full blast being directed at them.

For example, if you decided to give an assembly or classroom talk on the Prodigal Son, then you should consider explaining or replacing the following words or concepts.

1. Inheritance – Explain that this is what the son receives when the father dies but he wanted it now. He valued his father's riches more than his father.

2. He shared it between them – Luke 15:12 explains that both sons received their share. It is good to just mention this as some children will think the elder son was treated unfairly.
3. Squandered – few children would understand this word. Wasted, would be better.

4. Sinned – A short explanation of what sin is would be helpful. Highlight the fact that when we sin it is because we all have a sin nature that seeks to do what we want and not what God wants. At this stage you could emphasise the younger son knew he had sinned against God.

5. Worthy – Deserve, would be understood by children. At this point you could highlight the fact that the younger son hoped, at best, to be his father's servant.

6. Robe, ring, and shoes – I would suggest that you just mention the three items as gifts that indicated membership of the family. Everyone would know he was a son.

7. Killed the fatted calf – Some people baulk at the fact animals are killed so, in this instance, I state that they had a great feast with the best of food.

8. Older son's jealousy – Having proved that he was treated well by his loving father, you can mention he did not have the same compassion and mercy as his father.

9. Devoured your property with prostitutes – For obvious reasons I would omit this statement by the oldest son.

10. Celebrate the lost and found – Conclude with teaching that this parable tells us about the heart of God. A moral application that we should be willing to forgive and restore those who have wronged us is good but do highlight that no matter what we have done we can turn to God, being sorry for our sin and asking Him for forgiveness. He promises to receive all who come to Him because Jesus paid the penalty for our wrongdoing.

If the school knows you are there as a Christian, then there should be no surprise that you teach from the Bible. Holding a Bible in your hand as you speak shows to everyone the source of your material. I use a battered and highlighted Children's Bible that I sometimes get a volunteer to read from.

It is appropriate to think about terms that you would avoid. Some Bible terms are completely foreign to many primary school children and, unless you have the time to explain them, it is wiser to think of alternative words or phrases.

Instead of saying, "God the Father was propitiated by the death of His Son", you could say, "The death of the Lord Jesus completely satisfied God's justice". As an alternative to saying, "And it repented the LORD that He had made man on the earth," you could say, "The LORD felt sorry that He had made man on the earth".

Although I would often mention that there is a consequence for wrongdoing, I would not willingly, in a school assembly or classroom, use the word 'Hell' as that could quickly raise objections to your visit. If, in a classroom setting, I am asked a question about Hell, then I will answer honestly and tell children that the Bible does teach about that place of eternal punishment for sin. Prefacing my teaching with words like, "The Bible teaches ..." or "Christianity teaches ..." means I have never experienced a problem with clear but gracious instruction on any subject.

Experience has taught me that some children can remember the smallest detail of what was said to them. Therefore, we need to ensure that we get any small details we do mention right, as well as teaching the big theme.

You may have noticed that I wrote, "any small details *we do mention*". The presumption behind that statement is the assumption that every detail that we know about a Bible story will not be mentioned at an assembly or in the classroom.

If you were telling the children about the 'Feeding of the 5,000', you might emphasise the Lord's ability to satisfy along with His compassion and power. Although you will probably tell the children the people sat down in groups of 50 and there were 12 baskets of leftovers, it would not be beneficial to give teaching on why there were groups of 50 or why there were 12 baskets. You might think that would also not be very beneficial for adults let alone children but that's another discussion!

They must discover and decide what is true."

Schoolchildren have frequently asked me, "What about other religions?" I will always state that we must respect the fact that people can have their own belief but that does not mean we are all correct. In most of these situations I will quote the words of the Lord Jesus, *"I am the way, the truth, and the life. No one comes to the Father except through Me"* (John 14:6) showing that He taught there was only one way to a right relationship with God, and that was through Him. Every child who can think logically has understood that if someone else says there is a different way to God then one of those beliefs must be wrong. They must discover and decide what is true.

We live in a culture where the topic of hate-speech has been highlighted, but whenever I have said that expressing a different belief to someone else or even saying that they are wrong does not imply that I hate them, every child has accepted that fact. Of course, times change, and wisdom is required. Someone once said, "If someone asks you the time, then you do not tell them how to make a watch", meaning that it can be wise to answer the question with minimum words and not go beyond what was directly asked.

However the servant of the Lord must not deceive people by distorting the truth. Recall the words of the Lord to Jeremiah.

"All the words that I command you to speak to them. Do not diminish a word" (Jeremiah 26:2b).

In your verbal communication be careful that the talk is not merely a lesson on good moral living but that it does point the listener to the one true God and the person and work of the Lord Jesus Christ.

Visual communication

The gospel is a verbal proclamation of God's great plan of salvation, so words are essential but the use of visual aids when speaking to children has, for decades, been seen as beneficial.
It is important to remember that whatever we use must be an aid. It should be there to assist the children to understand the lesson that you are giving. If the visual aid becomes the thing that they remember rather than the point it was used to highlight, then the aid has not achieved its purpose.

There are many different visual aids that can be used to help teach a Bible lesson.

Some people have invested a great deal of time to learn ventriloquism. Primary school children love seeing and listening to the interaction between the ventriloquist and the dummy. A lot of patience and time will be required to be proficient in this art but there are a lot of internet resources that can be used if an individual desires to progress down this route. I do admire the skill and patience of those who have pursued this route but recognise it is a very narrow way and not many will travel on it.

Years ago flannelgraphs were a widely used resource. The basic idea was that the lesson could be given by using a felt background that had been placed on an easel. Flannel figures could then be placed on the background and moved as the lesson progressed. Practice in moving scenes and figures is essential if this method is to be used. Due to the size limitations the flannelgraph would not be suitable for large crowds, but it can still be very effective in smaller groups (up to 50-60 children). Youngsters who have been raised in an era of electronic technology could find this presentation method to be captivating and refreshing. Flannelgraph resources can be found at www.bettylukens.com/.

Another older presentation method is by Flash Cards. A Bible lesson is presented by showing a series of drawings, usually in a spiral bound folder, to a small group of young children. Once again, this method is not suitable for a large group but could be used for a small group (up to 20-30 children) in a classroom setting. Flashcards are not commonly used today but can be found at Child Evangelism Fellowship stores (www.cefireland.com/shop/).

A ministry called Foundation Matters offers a comprehensive flash card set with 38 Bible Stories on 237 A3 Flashcards at store.foundationmatters.org/product/creation-to-christ/.

Using an object or objects can be a very efficient way to present a Bible lesson. As mentioned previously, I have a small black bag containing objects (Bread, Torch, Mirror, Sword etc) that are used to describe the Bible. After giving a clue, I ask the children to guess what object is in the bag. Once they guess, I then tell them how that pictures a feature of the Bible (Food for the soul, light for the path, mirror that reveals us, sword that can penetrate and defend us).

If you do not mind a bit of acting, then how about presenting the lesson in the first person pretending that you were there? Obviously, you will inform the children that you are playing a role and that you are not an actual witness from over 2,000 years ago. This alternative presentation method can work very well for certain lessons. Imagine telling the events, through the eyes of Isaac, when Abraham took him up the mountain as a sacrifice. Maybe Isaac, when lying on the altar, recalled the words of his father to the servants, "We will come back to you". In playing the role of Isaac, you could really build the tension and then explain the great lesson that comes from those events. The method that I most often use is a slideshow presentation from a laptop onto a large screen. The most commonly used software for this is Microsoft PowerPoint but other software is available. Those of a certain age who remember acetates and overhead projectors (younger readers will need to Google those words!) will surely be thankful that a lot of work has been removed with the advent of new technology. There are many sources of good pictures that can be used to aid in the presentation of a Bible lesson but here are four I have used:

1. John Ritchie www.ritchiechristianmedia.co.uk/ has a selection of PowerPoint presentations on a variety of Bible lessons and Missionary stories. Searching for 'Eikon Art' or 'Tales of Truth' will help you locate them on the website.

2. Free Bible Images www.freebibleimages.org/ provide a massive collection of images for virtually every Bible lesson. As the name suggests, the images are free to use and can be placed into your presentation.

3. Foundation Matters provide several presentations that are available at store.foundationmatters.org/.

4. For a small cost you can obtain over 1100 images of many Old and New Testament lessons at www.theglorystory.com/ product/bible-pictures/.

When you have a presentation, you can adapt it with your own text. I sometimes put key words on the images and frequently use speech bubbles with the words of Scripture coming from the character's mouth. If you do this, then consider what words the children will understand.

Undeniably, a PowerPoint presentation is the most widely used resource in school assemblies. Nearly every school I visit has a large screen and audio equipment. Depending on your proficiency (or any help you can get from others) then you could include video and audio into your assembly.

❚❚ Talk to the audience, not to the screen."

Although I have negligible musical ability, my assemblies frequently include singing. An audio file inserted onto a slide containing the words of a chorus can be used to great effect. Due to my lack of talent, I use easy catchy tunes and simple action choruses ("Take my hand and follow me", "God's love is the best love" etc) that children will easily learn and can sing along with. Those of greater musical ability will, of course, be able to have an expanded catalogue of songs and music to use.

Before we leave the subject of presenting using PowerPoint, I would like to offer a few points for successful presenting using this format:

1. Talk to the audience, not the screen. - The pictures and text are an aid, but you are the presenter. Although a quick glance to the screen is fine, you must know your presentation. A sure way to get children to lose interest in what you are saying is for you to stop looking at them. Staring at the back of your head as you look at the screen will quickly disengage them.

2. Do not overload the talk with loads of pictures. - This will help with point 1. Try and keep to a maximum of 10-12 slides. Too many pictures can mean that you get distracted in switching between slides and the presentation becomes too much of a focus rather than the words that you use.

3. If you use text, then have a minimum point size of 30 for the font. - It is pointless having text that people cannot read.

Body language

As we not only communicate with words but our bodies, it is useful to consider a few basic points.

Show some passion. If we do not show some passion when we talk, then the children will think we are not excited about the subject, and so they have no reason to get excited or believe it themselves. Although all of us have different personalities and we know God can work through the dullest preacher, it does not excuse a joyless and lifeless demeanour. So, seek to show your natural excitement for the great truths you are presenting. Be mindful though that "Painted fire never burns". People can discern when we are not being real.

Maintain eye-contact - Along with having passion a speaker must make eye-contact with the audience. This is a reason that you should not be looking at the screen. Do not stare at one person and keep a limit of 2-3 seconds for any individual contact. In a large room seek to engage all areas, front to back and side to side. If you look at them, you should be able to gauge if they have understood and if you need to clarify something you said.

Smile – Although you do not need to go through a whole assembly looking as though you have a coat hanger stuck in your mouth, having a smile on your face is important. People will see you as welcoming and friendly. Undoubtedly, some of the adults and children who listen to what you have to say will be unbelieving and/or sceptical but a friendly smile can help in building relational bridges.

CONCLUSION

If you have managed to read all this book before reaching this final chapter, then "WELL DONE". You have persevered to the end.

My goal was to share with the reader my experience, observations, and learnings in connecting the local church to the local schools. I would like to leave you with some encouragement.

I do hope and pray that it will be a stimulus and encouragement for you as you seek to engage with local schools in the community where the LORD has placed you.

Please remember that He has placed you in your location at this time for His purpose. Many years ago Paul instructed the Athenians that God determines our times and our place of habitation.

*"And He has made from one blood every nation of men to dwell on all the face of the earth, and **has determined their preappointed times and the boundaries of their dwellings**"* (Acts 17:26).

That lesson is unchanging, so do seek to serve where you are. It is no accident that you are where you are. He alone opens the doors of opportunity and will direct you, if you seek Him.

Additionally, due to the "instant 'want it now' culture" we can sometimes overestimate what can be achieved in a year but underestimate what can be achieved in five years. The call is to *"run with endurance the race that is set before us"* (Hebrews 12:1b). Look to the LORD when your ministry seems to be prospering and when it appears to be floundering. Your own assessment is possibly inaccurate, but you must know that He will reward your faithfulness to Him, and His work. Keep going in the work that He has called you to. He has promised to be with you and give you all that you need to do His will.

His purpose is for you to be where you are and for you to endure in your service for Him.

May God bless your work,

Paul Coxall

January 2023